P9-DFA-403

THE VALUE OF LEARNING

The Story of Marie Curie

VALUE COMMUNICATIONS, I
PUBLISHERS
LA JOLLA, CALIFORNIA

THE
VALUE
OF
LEARNING

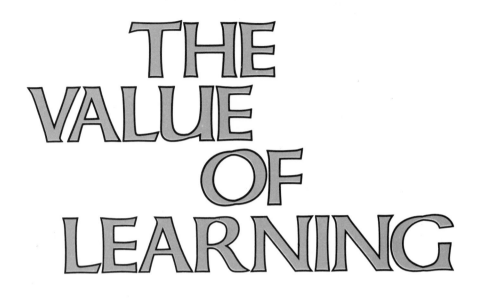

ILLUSTRATED BY Pileggi

The Story of
Marie Curie

BY ANN DONEGAN JOHNSON

The Value of Learning is part of the ValueTales series.

The Value of Learning text copyright © 1978 by Ann Donegan
Johnson. Illustrations copyright © 1978 by Value
Communications, Inc.

All rights reserved under International and Pan American
Copyright Conventions.
No part of this book may be reproduced in any manner
whatsoever without written permission from the publisher,
except in the case of brief quotations embodied in reviews
and articles.

First Edition
Manufactured in the United States of America
For information write to: ValueTales, P.O. Box 1012
La Jolla, CA 92038

Library of Congress Cataloging in Publication Data

Johnson, Ann Donegan.
    The value of learning.

    (ValueTales)
    SUMMARY: A brief biography emphasizing the
importance of learning in the life of the scientist who was
awarded the Nobel prize for her work in chemistry.
    1. Curie, Marie Sklodowska, 1867-1934—
Juvenile literature. 2. Chemists—Poland—
Biography—literature. [1. Curie, Marie
Sklodowska, 1867-1934. 2. Chemists. 3. Learning
—Psychology] I. Title.
QD22.C8J6   530′.092′4 [B] [92]   78-6433

ISBN 0-916392-18-X

Dedicated to Léonie and Mike

This tale is about a person who loved to learn, Marie Curie. The story that follows is based on events in her life. More historical facts about Marie Curie can be found on page 63.

Once upon a time...

in the city of Warsaw in the far-away country called Poland, there lived a little girl named Marya. In Polish, Marya means Mary.

Marya was very much like other little girls. In the evenings, she and her brother and sisters liked to sit around the fire and listen while their mother or their father read stories to them. Marya liked the stories, but what she really wanted to do was to learn to read by herself.

7

"You're only four, Marya," her parents told her. "That's much too young to worry about reading."

But Marya's sister Bronya, who was three years older, had wonderful cardboard cutouts of the letters of the alphabet. She used them to make words, and sometimes she made words especially for Marya.

"That's 'tree'!" Marya would cry. "Just like the tree we're sitting under!"

"You learn so quickly," Bronya would say.

"Do I?" said Marya. "I'm glad. It's fun to learn."

Of course Bronya could teach Marya simple words, like "tree" and "cat" and "mat." But she was only seven herself, and sometimes she had trouble with longer words.

One evening, when she was reading for her father and Marya, Bronya had so much trouble with the words that she wanted to stop. "Don't worry, Bronya," said her father. "Take your time. Read slowly and the words will come."

Marya was bright and curious. She was also very impatient. She grabbed Bronya's book and began to read.

"Marya, I can't believe it!" cried Bronya. "Did I teach you to do that? With those simple cardboard cutouts?"

Marya laughed. "I guess you must have," she said. "Isn't this fun? Now I can read by myself!"

11

Marya read from that day on, and she learned many things from books. She also learned by paying attention to the world around her, and by asking lots of questions.

Marya's father was a professor of science, and one day Marya stood on a chair in his laboratory and opened a cabinet. There were all sorts of bottles and jars inside the cabinet. "What are those?" Marya asked.

"They're tools that scientists use when they work," said her father.

"What kind of work do scientists do?" asked Marya.

"They find out about things," said her father.

Marya laughed. "I love to find out about things," she said. "Maybe one day I can be a scientist, too."

One day, when Marya was alone in the laboratory, she thought she heard a little voice call, "Hi there, Marya!"

Marya looked up and saw a little test tube standing on the cabinet shelf. "My name is Fizz," said the test tube, "and I'd like to talk with you." And with that, the test tube hopped down and landed beside Marya.

Of course Marya knew that test tubes don't come to life, but she decided to pretend that Fizz was real. She knew that if she talked with Fizz, she would really be talking with herself. Just the same, she thought it would be fun to have a make-believe friend who was a test tube.

"I notice that you like it here in the laboratory, Marya," said Fizz. "Perhaps one day you'll be a scientist and have a laboratory of your own."

"Wouldn't that be wonderful?" said Marya. "But so many people say that girls can't be scientists."

"If you learn enough, you can do almost anything you want to do," said Fizz. "It doesn't matter whether you're a girl or a boy."

Marya liked the things Fizz told her, so when she was old enough to go away to school, she took Fizz with her.

Russia ruled Poland in those days, and the Russians insisted that the Polish people learn Russian history. They ordered that all Poles should speak Russian, and they sent Russian soldiers to the schools to make sure that the children did not study Polish history.

"How terrible!" said Fizz. "People should be able to learn the history of their own people."

Now the teachers liked to outwit the Russians, so the little girls in Marya's school all had Polish history books. When it was time for a lesson in Polish history, they took out their books. One little girl watched at the window to warn the class if a Russian soldier was coming to the school.

"This is more like it," said Fizz happily.

Marya was excited. It was fun to study Polish history, and it was fun to watch out for the Russian soldiers.

One day the little girl who watched at the window heard the clump, clump, clump of boots on the street outside. A Russian soldier was marching toward the school.

"He's coming! He's coming!" cried the girl. "It's a Russian soldier and he's almost here!"

"Oh dear!" said the teacher. "Quickly! Hide your history books!"

The girls dashed this way and that as they ran to find hiding places for their books. They bumped into each other and tripped over each other, and one of them stumbled and sent Fizz flying across the room.

"Hurry! Please hurry!" said the teacher.

The Russian soldier tramped into the room. He saw a group of well-behaved little girls who were doing needlework. Some of them were a bit out of breath, but he didn't notice that.

"Very good!" said the Russian. He turned to the teacher. "Mistress, have one of your girls tell me the names of all the czars—in Russian!"

Some of the little girls began to tremble, for there had been a great many czars of Russia. Then Marya heard the teacher calling her name.

"Oh, dear," thought Marya. "I hope I don't make a mistake."

Marya began to recite the names of the czars, beginning with the very first one. She knew them all, and she listed them off in perfect Russian.

"Whew!" thought Fizz. "It's a darn good thing Marya knows all those Russian names!"

Marya knew a great deal more than the names of the czars by the time she reached high school. She enjoyed learning things, and when she was sixteen she graduated from high school first in her class.

"Isn't that great?" crowed Fizz.

Marya's father certainly thought it was great. "You've worked very hard at school," he told Marya. "Now you must have a reward. I'm sending you to visit your cousins in the country."

Marya loved being in the country. She took Fizz along with her, and on nice days they rode horseback across the green, open fields. "Whoa!" cried Fizz as they bounced along. "Take it easy, Marya."

In the evenings, Marya's cousins and their friends would have parties. They would sing and dance and have a wonderful time. Marya had such a good time that she wanted to dance all night.

Marya arrived home from the country to find that Bronya was very sad. "I do so want to go to medical school in Paris," said Bronya, "but I can't. We don't have the money."

"I'm afraid a professor's job doesn't pay very well," said their father.

Marya thought about this for a minute. Then she put her arms around Bronya. "We can manage!" she said. "I'll get a job and send you the money you need."

"You?" said Bronya. "But . . . but what can you *do*?"

"I can be a governess and teach little children," answered Marya.

"But you've always wanted to go to the university yourself," protested Bronya.

"And I *will* go," Marya declared. "I'll send you money until you finish your studies. Then, once you're a doctor, you can help me!"

25

Marya found a job with a very nice family who lived far
away from Warsaw. She enjoyed teaching, and the
children in the family liked their lively young governess.
She could play hide and seek with them and make them laugh.

Of course, Fizz went with Marya, and he always
reminded her that one day she would go to the university
and become a scientist. So, when she had a moment to
herself, Marya continued to read and study and learn.

After five long, patient years, Marya received a very special letter from her father. "My dear Marya," said the letter. "I have a new job that pays very well. I can send Bronya money for her studies, so you don't have to work as a governess any longer. Please come home, for I miss you."

"Oh, Fizz!" cried Marya. "Isn't that wonderful! I can go home. I can see my father again. And maybe it will be my turn to go to the university before very long!"

When Marya arrived home, she rushed to her father and threw her arms around him. "At last!" she cried. "It's been such a long, long time."

"It's good to have you back, dear Marya," said her father. "The house has been empty without you."

Marya wanted to keep studying and learning while she waited for her turn to go to the university. But at that time it was not easy for Polish people to continue their educations after high school. The Russians felt that they could control Poland more easily if the Poles did not have too much learning. Poles who wished to study had to do so in secret.

Marya found friends who were interested in learning, and in the evenings they met at one another's homes. They studied together and exchanged information. But they had to keep changing their meeting place so as not to attract attention. It would have been dangerous if they had been caught.

Marya studied in this way for several months. Then one day a letter came from Paris. "It's from Bronya!" cried Marya. "She's finished medical school and she wants me to come and stay with her and her new husband Cashmir. Now I can go to the university at last!"

"I'm so happy for you, Marya," said her father. "You've certainly earned your chance to become a scientist."

30

"Aren't you glad you kept on with your studies?" said Fizz. "Now you can do what you've always wanted."

Indeed Marya was glad. "It's all been worthwhile," she whispered to Fizz.

"I know it will be hard work, but I don't care," said Marya. She ran upstairs to pack. "Hard work is fun when you're learning things, and if I become a great scientist and discover something important, it could help people."

"Stop daydreaming and hurry," warned Fizz. "You'll miss your train if you don't pay attention."

Marya hurried and finished her packing, and her father went with her to the railroad station.

Suddenly Marya felt terribly lonely. "Oh, Father, I'm going to miss you!" she cried.

"And I'll miss you, dear Marya," he said. "But you must go now. You gave your sister her chance to be a doctor. Now it's your turn to become a scientist."

So Marya and Fizz got on the train, and it chugged slowly out of the station and away from Warsaw.

By the time she reached Paris Marya wasn't sad any more.
She was happy and excited. Bronya and Cashmir were
waiting at the train station to meet her, and they laughed
when they saw how eager she was.

"Now we can go immediately to the Sorbonne!" she said.

"Don't you even want to go home first?" asked Bronya.

Marya didn't. The Sorbonne was one of the best universities in the world, and it was one of the few that accepted women in the science department in those days. Marya couldn't wait to see it. And when she registered for her classes, she decided that she would not use the name Marya any longer. "Now that I'm in Paris, I shall use the French name for Marya, which is Marie," she said. And from that day on she was called Marie.

SORBONNE

At first Marie was very happy with Bronya and Cashmir. But after her classes began, she had a problem.

"Oh, Fizz," she said one evening, "Bronya and Cashmir are wonderful people. They have so many friends who come to visit them and chatter and play the piano. How can I work with so much going on?"

"I'm not sure you can," said Fizz.

So Marie went to talk with Bronya and Cashmir.

"CHUC

"I love your home and I love your friends," said Marie. "You know such nice people. I enjoy them when I'm not studying. But when I'm trying to learn something, I just can't concentrate here. I think it would be better if I rented a small room near the university. Then I'd be close to the laboratory and the library, too."

"We understand, Marie," said Bronya. "We love having you stay with us, but you do need a quieter place."

"I think this move is for the best," said Fizz when Marie found a little attic room near the university.

But as time went by, Fizz wasn't so sure. Marie wanted to save coal and oil, so she studied each evening at the library. Then, when the library closed at ten o'clock, she came back to the chilly room, and she often studied on into the night. At last, when her hands were too cold to hold a pen and her eyes could no longer stay open, she would go to bed.

"Marie, you must get more rest," warned Fizz. "And you aren't eating enough. You'll be sick if you don't watch out."

Marie laughed, and she told Fizz she was too busy to worry about sleep and food. "There's so much to learn," she said.

But one evening Marie felt dizzy as she came in from the Sorbonne. She tried to climb the stairs to her room and she couldn't. She fell to the floor in a faint.

"Good night!" cried Fizz. "I was afraid of this!"

Fizz was terribly glad when one of Marie's classmates came along just then and found her.

Marie's friend sent for Cashmir, who was very upset when he found Marie so pale and shaky. "Marie, you look dreadful!" he cried. "You haven't been taking care of yourself. What have you been eating?"

"I'm not sure," whispered Marie. "I think I had some cherries and some radishes today."

"And I suppose you've been staying up very late at night studying?" questioned Cashmir.

Marie nodded sheepishly.

"Put on your coat!" ordered Cashmir. "You're coming home with me!"

"I hope you've learned your lesson, Marie," said Fizz, when Marie was safely in Bronya's home, eating a good meal.

Marie laughed. "I had almost forgotten how good food tasted," she said. "You're right, Fizz. It was silly of me to make myself sick. It won't do me any good to learn things if I don't have my health."

"Make sure you remember that," said Fizz.

Marie soon recovered, and she did remember how dreadful it felt to be ill. She took better care of herself, and she tried not to be impatient. "There's so much to learn if I'm to be a scientist," she told Fizz. "I can't do it overnight."

She went on working in the laboratory at the university. She loved it there. She loved the silence when people were intent on what they were doing. She loved the wonderful instruments and the gleaming test tubes and beakers.

After working in the laboratory for several years and going to lectures at the university, Marie knew a great deal about all kinds of scientific things. At last it was time for her to take the examination that would qualify her as a scientist. "I'm so nervous," she said. "I can't remember a thing."

"Just relax," whispered Fizz. "You'll do fine."

Fizz was right. Marie did so well on her examination that she was first in the whole class.

"Look, Fizz, now I'm *really* a scientist!" exclaimed Marie. "All the hard work was worth it."

"It *was* hard work, wasn't it?" said Fizz. "But it was fun, too."

"That's right," said Marie, "and there's lots more work ahead—and fun—because no matter how much I know, there will still be new things to learn."

45

Soon many people were asking Marie to do scientific work for them. One day a friend who was a professor dropped in to visit her in her little laboratory at the university. Marie was looking worried and upset.

"What's the matter, Marie?" asked her friend.

"I'm getting such interesting work to do," Marie told him, "but I don't have the right equipment. And even if I had the equipment, I don't have the space in this laboratory to use it."

"Hm!" said the professor. "You *do* seem to be a little crowded." He thought for a moment. Then he said, "I know someone who might be able to help you."

"You do?" said Marie. "That would be wonderful!"

WORK TO DO

Soon after that, Marie was invited to the professor's house to meet the well-known scientist Pierre Curie. Perhaps Marie felt a bit shy when she first met this famous man, but she liked him very much. And Pierre was very impressed with Marie, he admired her knowledge and her charm.

''What a charming, interesting young lady this is,'' thought Pierre Curie.

Then the professor told Pierre about Marie's tiny laboratory. ''She's doing some very important work,'' he said, ''but she doesn't have the proper equipment, and she doesn't have enough space.''

When Pierre heard this, he quickly asked Marie to come and work in his laboratory. "I'd be delighted to have you," he said.

"But I don't want to bother you," said Marie.

"You won't," Pierre assured her.

Fizz smiled. "I like Pierre Curie," he thought.

Marie was pleased to finally have a place big enough to do her important work. Pierre was glad to be able to help Marie. Each morning he looked forward to coming to work in his laboratory and seeing her.

Marie had known Pierre for only a few months when he asked her to marry him. "I love you very much," he told her. "I want to be with you always."

Marie felt very happy, but she was also troubled. "I love you, too," she told Pierre, "and I want to be with you. But sometimes I think I should return to my native Poland."

Pierre shook his head. "I know that you're homesick at times," he said, "but Poland is under Russian rule. You wouldn't be allowed to continue your work there."

What do you suppose Marie said then?

51

She said that she would marry Pierre.

Their wedding took place one year after Marie and Pierre met. Marie and Pierre were very happy on their wedding day. They had so much to look forward to. Being together, sharing their knowledge, and working with each other.

Fizz was quietly beaming.

Marie and Pierre were very happy indeed. On their honeymoon they bicycled out into the country, far from the hustle and bustle of Paris. Sometimes they stopped in a meadow and had a picnic lunch. Sometimes they gathered wildflowers for their room. Life was beautiful, and it was fun to be together.

After they returned from their honeymoon, Marie and Pierre continued to work together. There was so much to be discovered that they spent many hours in their laboratory. Then something happened that made their lives even more complete. Marie and Pierre had a baby daughter.

"She's so beautiful," exclaimed Marie looking into the baby's crib.

"She looks just like you," said Pierre. Marie smiled.

"Let's call her Irène," said Marie. Pierre agreed.

Marie enjoyed being a mother and she enjoyed being a scientist. She did a wonderful job of each.

In these years, flat glass plates that were used for photographs were kept wrapped in black paper so that they would not develop white spots from being exposed to rays of light. Marie learned that another scientist had placed certain rocks near some wrapped photographic plates and that the plates had then unexpectedly developed white spots. That meant that the rocks were giving off rays—invisible rays so powerful that they could fight their way through the black paper. The scientist called these x-rays. "I wonder," said Marie, "what substance could be in those rocks to give off such rays."

Marie, with Pierre's help, began to study these unusual rocks. She then went on to study other rocks and found another type that also gave off invisible rays. This rock was called pitchblende. It was black and hard.

"There must be some substance in this rock that we don't know about," said Marie. "One rock has very little of this substance that gives off the rays. If I could get a lot of pitchblende rocks and boil them down, perhaps I could produce enough of whatever the substance is so that I could actually see the rays."

"But pitchblende is very expensive," said Fizz. "How can you get a lot of it?"

As it turned out, Marie was very lucky. The emperor of Austria learned about her work, and he sent her a ton of pitchblende as a gift. So Marie and Pierre got a big pot and they boiled down the pitchblende, little by little. Each time they boiled a rock it would melt down until only a very little bit was left.

One night, two years after they first began boiling down the pitchblende, Pierre and Marie went into their laboratory to check on their experiment.

"Pierre, look!" cried Marie.

What they saw was a beautiful, shimmering radiant blue glow coming from the pot. They had finally boiled enough pitchblende to be able to see the rays they were looking for.

"Wonderful!" said Pierre. "Now the entire world will be able to see the rays—rays that we thought existed but that no one has ever seen before."

Marie later decided to call the substance inside the pitchblende that produced the blue rays *radium*.

When Marie and Pierre discovered radium, they actually discovered a new chemical element, which is a very difficult thing to do. It is a marvelous thing to discover a new element, for the elements are the materials out of which our universe is made.

Marie and Pierre received many honors because of their work. One was especially dear to them. It was the Nobel prize for physics, which was presented to them by the king of Norway.

While the prizes pleased them, they were much, much more pleased when they found out about the ways radium could be used. With the help of rays from this element, scientists could see through things, and even through people. Radium could be used to test diamonds to see if they were real. Most important, radium could cure certain types of cancer. Because of Marie's discovery, many lives have been saved.

Because she loved learning, Marie Curie reached her goal. She became a famous scientist, and she was able to help many people. If you want to be the one to decide what you will do with your life, maybe learning will help you discover what you want to do and help you reach your goal.

The End

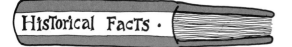

Marie Curie was born Marya Sklodowska on November 7, 1867, in Warsaw, Poland. Over one hundred years before Marya's birth, Poland had been overrun by its stronger neighbors and divided into German, Russian, and Austrian sections. Marya was born in the Russian part of Poland. Attempts at revolt by the Polish people made the Russians intent on suppressing Poland's religion, books, newspapers, and even the national language. When Marya was a young girl, the Polish heroes were those who taught the younger generation and who helped them hold on to their Polish heritage. Learning was a privilege then, not a right.

From childhood, Marya was known for her extraordinary memory. She learned to read at the age of four. Seven years later, Marya's mother died of tuberculosis and her father was left to raise four children by himself. He was a professor of mathematics and physics. And he kept a glass case in the house filled with his scientific instruments—glass tubes, small scales, and an electroscope. Marya was fascinated with the instruments and hoped that one day she, too, would be a scientist.

Marya was educated in Russian schools by Polish teachers and was considered "remarkably gifted." At sixteen she graduated from a Russian secondary school first in her class. Because her father did not have much money, Marya took a job as a governess to help pay for her sister Bronya's education at the Sorbonne University in Paris. Their understanding was that once Bronya became a doctor she would help pay for Marya's education. In 1891 Marya finally went to Paris and enrolled as a student in the Faculty of Science at the Sorbonne. She signed her registration card using the French translation of Marya, "Marie."

With a passion to learn everything she possibly could, Marie worked far into the night and for weeks would live on nothing but bread and butter, fruit and tea. She earned the Licence of Physical Sciences in 1893, passing first in her class, and the Licence of Mathematical Sciences in 1894, passing second in her class. It was in the beginning of that year that Marie met the French physicist Pierre Curie. Their marriage, based on love and admiration, was also to become a scientific partnership that would receive

MARIE CURIE
1867–1934

worldwide recognition for their joint achievements. The birth of their two daughters (Irène, 1897 and Ève, 1904) did not interrupt Marie's scientific work. She was determined to be both a mother and a scientist, and she succeeded at both.

In 1896, Henri Becquerel discovered that uranium salts emitted rays similar to x-rays in their penetrating power. The Curies studied this new phenomenon—which Marie later named radioactivity—to see if substances other than uranium also emitted these rays. In 1903, Marie earned her doctorate in physics. That same year the Curies shared, with Henri Becquerel, the Nobel prize in physics for their investigations of uranium and radioactive materials.

In 1906 Pierre Curie was run over and killed on a Paris street. Marie then directed all her energies toward her work and succeeded Pierre as director of the physics laboratory at the Sorbonne. She was the first woman to teach there.

In 1911 the Swedish Academy of Sciences awarded Marie Curie the Nobel prize in chemistry for her discovery of the elements radium and polonium. She was the only person ever to have received the Nobel prize in both physics and chemistry.

On July 4, 1934, Marie died of pernicious anemia caused by her long exposure to radium. She left behind a tremendous contribution to the world of science that continues to influence the work of today's physicists and chemists.

The ValueTale Series